D0434925

The Pig of Happiness

for Sarah

06 07 08 09 10 RR6 10 9 8 7 6 5 4 3 2 1

ISBN-13: 978-0-7407-6373-1
ISBN-10: 0-7407-6373-3

www.edwardmonkton.com

www.andrewsmcmeel.com

ATTENTION: SCHOOLS AND BUSINESSES
Andrews McMeel books are available at quantity
discounts with bulk purchase for educational, business, or
sales promotional use. For information, please write to: Special
Sales Department, Andrews McMeel Publishing, LLC,
4520 Main Street, Kansas City, Missouri 64111.

THE PIG OF HAPPINESS

Edward Monkton

Andrews McMeel
Publishing, LLC
Kansas City

There was once
a PIG

He was an ORDINARY
PIG in all ways

But one thing did
SET him APART

This thing was his DISTASTE for the MUMBLING and GRUMBLING that is the Natural Way with pigs

... thought the PIG

I shall become an

EXTRAORDINARY

PIG !

From now on I shall
Stand for everything
that is

LIGHT ☼

and

BEAUTIFUL ✿

and TRUE ♡

and

WONDERFUL

I shall see the BEST
in EVERYONE

and the BEST
in EVERYTHING

I shall become . . .

THE PIG
of HAPPINESS!

and so it did come to pass

The next day, when Pig A COMPLAINED about the weather...

The Pig of Happiness went
DANCING in the rain

The day after that, when
Pig B was RUDE about
Pig C's bottom and all the
other pigs joined in...

The Pig of Happiness gave
Pig C a FLOWER and
said in front of all the other
pigs that he thought Pig C
had a BEAUTIFUL bottom
actually

And so it continued daily

After a while, the Pig of Happiness became so HAPPY with being happy that his HAPPINESS became too BIG

It had to find an ESCAPE

And so it was that it began to LEAK and SEEP from inside him into all the OTHER pigs

Now ALL the pigs are
HAPPY

And their HAPPINESS
is beginning to show signs
of LEAKING too

The SHEEP are LAUGHING

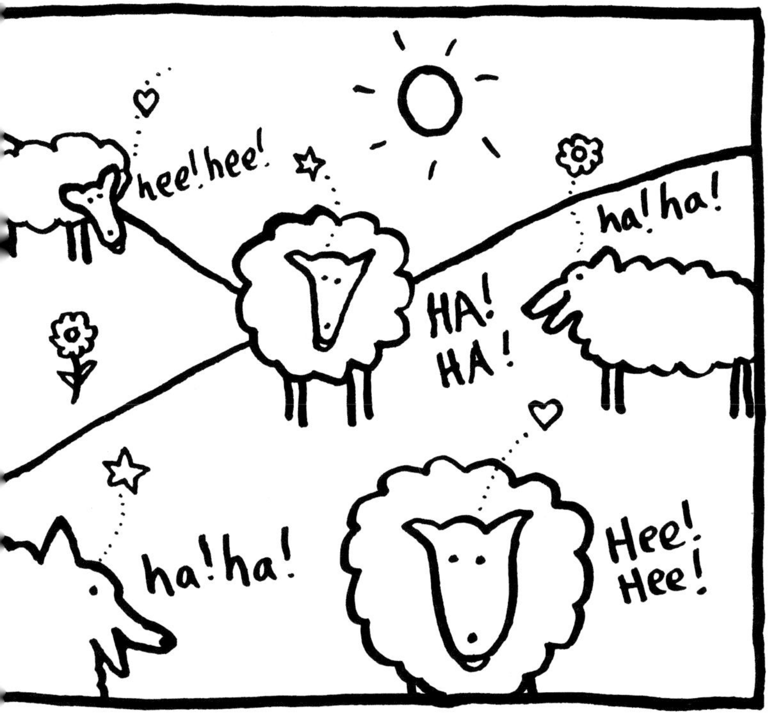
hee! hee!
ha! ha!
HA! HA!
ha! ha!
Hee! Hee!

Even the CHICKENS
are beginning to
SMILE

THE END